CONTENTS

Front endpaper: *Corydoras paleatus.* Photo by H. J. Richter.

Frontis: Common angelfish, *Pterophyllum scalare.* Photo by Klaus Paysan.

Back endpaper: A firemouth cichlid, *Cichlasoma meeki,* tending to its brood. Photo by H.J. Richter.

ISBN 0-87666-512-1 • KW-026

© Copyright 1980 by T.F.H. Publications, Inc.

Distributed in the UNITED STATES by T.F.H. Publications, Inc., 211 West Sylvania Avenue, Neptune City, NJ 07753; in CANADA by H & L Pet Supplies Inc., 27 Kingston Crescent, Kitchener, Ontario N2B 2T6; Rolf C. Hagen Ltd., 3225 Sartelon Street, Montreal 382 Quebec; in ENGLAND by T.F.H. Publications Limited, 4 Kier Park, Ascot, Berkshire SL5 7DS; in AUSTRALIA AND THE SOUTH PACIFIC by T.F.H. (Australia) Pty. Ltd., Box 149, Brookvale 2100 N.S.W., Australia; in NEW ZEALAND by Ross Haines & Son, Ltd., 18 Monmouth Street, Grey Lynn, Auckland 2 New Zealand; in SINGAPORE AND MALAYSIA by MPH Distributors Pte., 71-77 Stamford Road, Singapore 0617; in the PHILIPPINES by Bio-Research, 5 Lippay Street, San Lorenzo Village, Makati, Rizal; in SOUTH AFRICA by Multipet Pty. Ltd., 30 Turners Avenue, Durban 4001. Published by T.F.H. Publications Inc., Ltd., the British Crown Colony of Hong Kong. THIS IS THE 1983 EDITION.

AQUARIUM FISH

U. ERICH FRIESE

The appearance of small round-ish fishes such as tiger barbs (left) is enhanced in a smaller tank that is high from top to bottom. Photo courtesy of Mr. and Mrs. Werther Paccagnella. Fishes such as bala sharks and gouramis (below) that are more elongate in shape look better in an elongated aquarium. Photo by Dr. D. Terver, Nancy Aquarium, France.

Introduction

One of the most pleasurable sights in a home, doctor's or dentist's office, or even in a restaurant, is an attractive aquarium filled with colorful exotic fishes, which provide a unique and esthetic viewing pleasure. Yet, such a picture of apparent harmony and tranquility can be deceptive to those who may become inspired to set up such an aquarium in their home. Unless the budding aquarist does his "homework" *before* he or she embarks on this new venture, much disappointment can lie in its path, which can easily destroy the initial enthusiasm.

These comments are not meant to discourage, but instead to lead the newcomer to the aquarium hobby onto the right path so that he is spared disappointment and the loss of money. Some preliminary reading on the various topics of simple aquarium management, together with a discussion of some of the more popular and hardier exotic fishes, can indeed make the difference between success and failure and thus provide immense enjoyment as opposed to disappointment. This little book is intended to provide this information within the framework of a concise summary of all that you need to know in order to succeed with the very first aquarium.

WHAT IS AN AQUARIUM?

An aquarium is a small confined body of water in which (usually) an extraordinarily large number of live aquatic organisms are being kept. For these organisms (which are usually fishes) the aquarium then becomes their total environment. Within this (confined) environment water is the highway and byway. In short, it provides simultaneously accommodation, food and board, drink, toilet and ultimately the grave of fishes. In fact, all of the fishes' vital functions of feeding, digestion, growth and reproduction are dependent on water. Therefore, when we set up an aquarium these are the factors that have to be kept in mind. In nature, where fishes usually live in large bodies of water (lakes, rivers, ponds), nature itself provides many regulating mechanisms to assure the survival of fishes. However, in an aquarium we can do so only with the help and support of some basic aids, which are essential if our fishes are to survive. These aids (equipment) are geared to accommodate the basic needs of fishes, which is to assure their survival. What are these basic needs? The most important aspects of the aquatic environment for fish are dissolved oxygen, dissolved salts, light, temperature, toxic substances, concentration of disease organisms and the opportunity to escape predators. The aquarist must cater to these demands by providing a sufficiently large tank, equipped with certain basic but essential technical equipment, in which we maintain the proper relationship between the numbers and sizes of fishes in the tank and their specific requirements.

THE AQUARIUM

Basically, there are three different points that have to be considered before the aquarium is purchased and set up in the home. 1) The prime consideration is the size of the tank. Here we have to remember what has been said above, that is, it is the *total* environment for the fishes. If too small a tank is selected, it will quickly be overcrowded. AN AQUARIUM CAN EASILY BE TOO SMALL, BUT IT CAN NEVER BE TOO LARGE. Although pet shops offer an abundance of oddly shaped small goldfish bowls, a community tank for tropical freshwater fishes should never be smaller than 10 gallons (smaller tanks are sometimes used for specific breeding purposes, but they should not be used as a community tank). Ideally such tanks should be made entirely out of glass in order to avoid the effects of any metallic corrosion. Some of the older style stainless steel tanks can also be used provided that they are made of high quality stainless steel. Unfortunately, many of these tanks do rust after all, and thus ugly brown spots appear on their once shiny frame. 2) Modern all-glass tanks are made of five pieces of glass, four sides and a bottom, glued together by a silicone sealant which does not give off any toxic substances into the water. Although such a tank can easily be built to any size, beginning aquarists should stick to commercially available models. These are made in standard sizes to fit a wide variety of standardized accessories. 3) All-glass tanks come in two different types: high and low. In the first category the height is the largest dimension, thus giving a reduced surface area. Since the amount of sur-

1

2

10

(1) For easy viewing, an aquarium should be located at eye level from a sitting position. Photo by J. Elias. (2) Rocks can be as decorative as green plants. Photo by Dr. D. Terver, Nancy Aquarium, France. (3) To mount an aquarium on a mantelpiece requires that the tank be long and narrow. Photo by L'Arche de Noe. (4) Decorated aquaria make excellent room dividers. Photo courtesy of Mr. and Mrs. Werther Paccagnella.

3

4

face area is very important in the absorption of vital oxygen from the air (remember the basic need of dissolved oxygen for fishes), this tank design should be rejected in favor of the latter low tank. Here the length (or width) provides the largest dimension and so gives a maximum surface area relative to the depth of the tank.

LOCATION OF THE AQUARIUM

Some thought should be given to this point because once a tank is put into a particular place and set up, decorated and filled with water it is very difficult to move it again, especially when it is a large tank. Firstly, an aquarium should not be placed in front of a window with direct (southerly) exposure to sunlight. Such a position would promote an excessive growth of algae, which not only looks unattractive but also causes considerable aquarium "housekeeping" problems. Since we are dealing with tropical fishes, which should be kept at a reasonably stable temperature, it is also important that the tank not be placed in a cold draft (stairway, hallway entrance, etc.). Similarly, warm air (from a close-by radiator or hot-air louver) can be equally harmful. Fishes are very sensitive to movements around their tank, but they do adjust readily to people walking around the tank. If we place the tank in a room where there is rarely any movement, the fishes tend to hide whenever someone comes into the room.

Once the proper location has been selected it is also important to determine whether the floor will support the weight of a tank. Such a consideration is, of course, relatively unimportant when one deals with a single 10-gallon tank. However, larger tanks should be carefully placed keeping the load-bearing capacity of the floor in mind. Here it has to be remembered that a cubic foot of water weighs 62.43 lbs. (= 7.48 gallons; 10 gallons = 83.46 lbs.; 20 gallons = 166.9 lbs., etc.).

FILTRATION

We saw at the beginning of this book that all vital functions of fishes, such as feeding and digestion, are dependent upon water. An aquarium is then effectively an accommodation, toilet and grave for the fishes in it. Consequently, there is a continuous accumulation of visible (debris, leftover food, etc.) and invisible (dissolved organic waste products) dirt in the aquarium. If this is permitted to accumulate it will quickly reach toxic levels and, therefore, it has to be removed regularly. A siphon hose will take out much, if not all, of the large debris (uneaten food, feces, artifacts, etc.), but the invisible components (the dissolved waste products) have to be removed with the aid of continuous filtration. This can be accomplished through a sub-gravel filter or a wide variety of commercially available outside fiters (from simple air-lift filters to high volume motor-driven power filters). All of these devices move water through a filter medium (sand and gravel with a sub-gravel filter; various inert materials, including charcoal, in outside filters), where a specific bacterial action purifies the water.

The beginning aquarist is best advised to use a simple sub-gravel filter. These plastic panels are placed on the bottom of the tank below a 2- to 3-inch layer of medium to fine gravel (or coarse sand). The filter stems are then connected to an air pump (wide variety of models and prices available) which then lifts water through the filter stem and so creates a continuous flow of water through the gravel (substrate). There large particles are then retained and, together with the dissolved waste products, are utilized by some highly specific bacteria located in the gravel.

AERATION

Since fishes have to remove dissolved oxygen from the water in order to live, the aquarium water would soon be depleted of this vital substance unless we, as aquarists, make sure that it is constantly replenished. If sub-gravel

1   2

3

In terms of their behavior, there are good and bad combinations of fishes for aquaria. Long-finned guppies (1) are relatively slow swimmers compared to zebra danios (2) and therefore cannot compete very well with the zebras for food. Photo 1 by A. Noznov; photo 2 by H.J. Richter. (3) Long-finned zebra danios will freely interbreed with normal zebra danios and therefore should not be mixed with them in a breeding tank if one wishes to keep the long-finned strain relatively pure. Photo by J. Elias. (4) No aquarium for smaller fishes should be without at least a few *Corydoras* catfishes. These fishes are strictly bottom feeders and do an excellent job of picking up leftover food that other fishes in the tank may miss. In addition, they root leftover food particles out of the surface gravel, thus preventing undergravel filters from plugging up. Photo by H.J. Richter.

filtration is being used, the air which pushes the water up the filter stems also tends to provide some of this dissolved oxygen. However, more importantly the movement of water created along the surface by filtration allows more atmospheric oxygen to be absorbed at the very thin interface where water and air meet. In addition, if live plants are in the tank these too will produce oxygen when exposed to light (while absorbing the carbon dioxide given off by the fishes during their respiration). However, aquarists have to be cautioned here, because these very same plants also use dissolved oxygen during the night and so place an additional stress (oxygen demand) on the aquarium water.

HEATING

Tropical fishes require water temperatures which range from about 20 °C to 26 °C. Some can routinely tolerate slightly higher or lower temperatures. Therefore, in most parts of the country the water will have to be heated, at least during the cold winter months. This can be done by placing the tank in a room with a more or less constant temperature of about 23 °C or higher or by using any of a variety of commercially available electrical immersion heaters. These are rod-shaped glass tubes with an electrical heating element. Most of the better aquarium heaters have a thermostat built in, which keeps the water temperature at a near-constant level. The heaters are small and compact, and so they can be hidden easily in a far corner of the aquarium or if the submersible type, behind a rock or other piece of tank decoration. The temperature requirements of tropical fishes vary; i.e., some require higher temperatures than others. Details of this will be discussed together with the requirements for specific fishes later on in this book.

LIGHTING

When selecting the location for the tank remember that strong direct sunlight has already been discouraged.

Moreover, sunlight is far too variable to provide consistently constant illumination for the tank, particularly when the hobbyist wants to enjoy his fish in the evening. Consequently, artificial illumination has to be provided through electric lighting, preferably in the form of an enclosed fitting on top of the tank. Such lighting units can be made of stainless steel or plastic and bought commercially (if the tank is of a standard commercial size). The actual light source is, nowadays, usually a fluorescent light. These come in different types and specific bulbs can be selected to enhance the color of your fishes and/or to promote water plant growth. Many hobbyists prefer bulbs of the "Grow-Lux" type, which delivers large amounts of red and blue rays. This type encourages plant growth and emphasizes red and blue colors, particularly those of iridescent fishes such as neon tetras. Yet some aquarists feel that this type of lighting gives the aquarium a garish, artificial appearance.

THE WATER

Most tropical fishes live in a soft, slightly acid to neutral water, whereas in an aquarium they usually encounter hard, slightly alkaline water, since in most parts of the country our water is very much different in its chemical makeup. Details about water chemistry go beyond the scope of this book, but such details can be found in some of the more comprehensive books.

Hardness

In nature no water is chemically pure, but instead it includes numerous substances which have become dissolved in it from the bottom substrate (soil) and the surrounding land mass. To a large degree these substances are salts of the element calcium and to a lesser degree of magnesium, forming carbonates and sulphates. Water with a high content of these substances is referred to as being hard, and

¹ All of the fishes shown above and on the opposite page are small, peaceful species that can get along well in the same aquarium. Their water chemistry and temperature requirements are about the same and are not particularly stringent. (1) The male (upper fish) cherry barb, *Capoeta titteya,* is especially colorful when kept in spawning condition. (2) *Rasbora maculata* reaches only an inch in length and is one of the prettiest of the *Rasbora* species. (3) The rummy-nose tetra, *Hemigrammus rhodostomus,* derives its common name from its red snout. Photos 1, 2 and 3 by H.J. Richter. (4) *Hyphessobrycon serpae* is one of the most colorful of the small characoids and is an extremely hardy species. Photo by R. Zukal.

water with a low calcium and magnesium content is known as soft water. Many of the more common exotic tropical fishes are very tolerant of the hardness, but a few are very sensitive. While water hardness is a very important factor for breeding tropical fishes, it is of little consequence for merely keeping some of the more common species.

pH (acidity)

Dissolved substances in water can have a profound effect upon the disassociation of the individual water molecules. They can create an excess of hydrogen (H+) ions, causing an increased acidity of the water, or an abundance of hydroxide (OH-) ions, causing the water to be alkaline. The (numerical) relationship between these two conditions is expressed as the pH value. For most tropical fishes it should be slightly on the acidic side (i.e., have a value slightly below pH 7, the neutral point). Hard water almost always has a pH between 7 and 8, whereas soft rain-forest water usually has a pH between 6 and 7 but often also considerably lower (than 7). For details about determining, maintaining and/or adjusting the pH a more comprehensive text must be consulted.

FURNISHING THE AQUARIUM

In most cases water plants provide the main form of interior decorating for the aquarium, that is if the fishes will tolerate plants (there are plant-eating fishes and those which tend to continuously uproot plants). The selection of plants and their arrangement in community tanks, where a number of fishes from different parts of the world are being kept together, is not really natural. However, invariably it is attractive and enhances the appearance of an aquarium. Among the commonly available and most suitable aquarium plants are the sword plants *(Echinodorus)*, *Vallisneria* species, *Aponogeton* species, *Cryptocoryne* species, *Cabomba* and *Myriophyllum*.

In addition to plants, the imaginative aquarist can also use artifacts such as wooden branches and tree roots (must be well water-logged; otherwise they float) and rocks and stones of different sizes.

In recent years there has also been a flood of artificial objects for use as aquarium decoration, such as earthenware or porcelain divers, treasure chests, shipwrecks, etc. Some of these items incorporate a hidden airstone, the most notorious among them being clam shells which open and release air bubbles trapped inside and water wheels driven by rising air bubbles. None of these items improve the aquarium conditions or increase the longevity of the fishes, and their esthetic value could be argued at great length.

AQUARIUM FISHES IN GENERAL

Every fish requires certain well-defined conditions of temperature, light, type of water, etc., so it can only live in those habitats where these conditions are present. Since environmental conditions vary greatly, sometimes even within a small geographical region, no single species of fish is found in all parts of the world. For the purpose of this book we are, of course, only concerned with those species of fishes which are small, colorful and occur in the tropical regions of the world. The largest number of fishes available in the pet trade came originally from tropical South America, although most of the fishes available nowadays are actually bred in captivity. In addition, large numbers of species have come from Malaysia, Vietnam, Cambodia, Thailand, and also from Africa. Australia has a very insignificant freshwater fauna and thus has made few contributions to the tropical fish trade. Because of their latitude with only a temperate climate, both North America and Europe have also provided only few forms which are of interest to home aquarists.

The tropical fish industry is very large, and every year numerous new fish species are being imported. However,

(1) The dwarf pencilfish, *Nannostomus marginatus*, is a good community tank species, but because of its small mouth, it must be given very small food particles. (2) *Pelvicachromis pulcher* is a good community tankfish if the other fishes in the tank are not smaller than about three inches in length, for like most cichlids, this fish can have a nasty temperament, especially during its spawning period. (3) The moss-green tiger barb is a mutant form of the normal tiger barb.(4) Keeping tiger barbs, *Capoeta tetrazona,* in a school of six to ten specimens will inhibit their tendency to nip at the fins of other fishes in the tank. Photos 1, 3 and 4 by H.J. Richter.

23

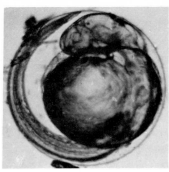

(1) Neon tetras
(Paracheirodon innesi), an
extremely popular aquarium
fish, are typical egg-
scatterers. With all egg-
scatterers the aquarist must
wait for the eggs (2) to
hatch and the larval fishes
to absorb the yolk sac
before the young fish begin
to swim free and feed ac-
tively. Photo 1 by R. Zukal.
Photo 2 by Dr. S. Frank.

most of these always disappear again because they are not
attractive enough, they are too difficult to keep or their
place of capture is too remote for collecting them in
economic proportions. Yet, over the years (since about the
turn of the century) a few have always remained and have
become established and popular among aquarists. This
eventually has led to the accumulation of a stable number
of species, a constant repertoire of classical aquarium
fishes, so to speak, of which the more popular ones and
those which are easy to keep in a home aquarium will be
presented in this book.

There are two major groups of fishes sold in the
aquarium hobby: livebearers and egglayers. The "livebearing" process among aquarium fishes is much different from
the "livebearing" process of mammals, but it is similar at
least in that an infant livebearer is a developed fish that

Within minutes of their birth, the young of livebearers such as guppies are ready to swim free and feed. Because of this almost "instant" reproduction, livebearers are traditionally very popular among novice aquarists. Photo by M. Chvojka.

looks like a fish. It is of course smaller and less colorful and less fully developed than its parents, but it is unmistakably a fish. It is not in an egg, and it doesn't have to hatch out and go through some sort of larval developmental stage before it's able to swim about and pursue the activities normal to its kind. The young of egglaying species, on the other hand, are not fully developed small fishes ready to swim about in their tank—they are laid in eggs, and before they are ready to swim freely they have to go through a developmental process the first step of which of course is to hatch out of the egg.

There are more egglaying species than livebearing species, and the egglaying species are classified within many different families of fishes, whereas the aquarium hobby's popular livebearing fishes are grouped within only one family.

Their smooth velvety black color and their ability to bear live young have made black mollies one of the most popular aquarium fishes of all time. Photo below by Dr. Herbert R. Axelrod.

Livebearers

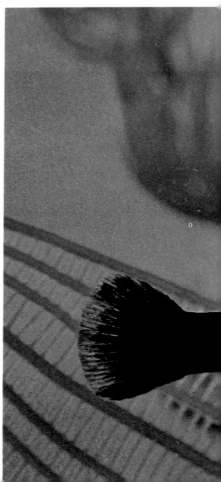

Livebearers are among the most easily kept tropical fishes. They are not particularly demanding in their care and do well under a variety of conditions, and so they are strongly recommended as fishes for beginning aquarists. There is an added incentive in keeping livebearers; they will invariably breed, even in a community aquarium (although special arrangements will have to be made for the young, otherwise these will be eaten by the other tank occupants).

Livebearing toothcarps make up a large family (Poeciliidae) consisting mainly of small fishes from Central

and South America. All members in this family give birth to live young by a unique process. The sperm fertilizing the eggs are introduced into the female by the gonopodium of the male (the transformed anal fin, which is highly movable). During the mating process the gonopodium is moved forward and passed into the genital opening of the female. In most species the eggs develop within the female so that the young have to break the egg membrane at birth or else they do so immediately afterwards. In many cases the female stores sperm for long periods of time so that several batches of young can be produced from one fertilization.

Many species and genera in this family are so closely related that they can cross-breed (hybridize), even in nature. The tropical fish industry has taken advantage of this by artificially producing a great variety of highly ornamental and colorful hybrids which are favorites among many aquarists. In fact, in one particular case special interest clubs have been formed solely dedicated to the propagation of a multitude of varieties of one particular species . . . the famous guppy.

THE GUPPY

Ever since the conception of the aquarium fish hobby, the guppy, *Poecilia reticulata,* has been its classic example. Since its first importation into Europe at the beginning of this century, the guppy has been one of the most popular aquarium fishes, not only because of its hardiness and willingness to readily breed in just about any size tank, but also because it is one of the most attractive tropical fishes.

Originally the guppy came from Venezuela, Barbados, Trinidad, Guyana and northern Brazil, but since then it has been introduced into many other tropical regions of the world. Its coloration is highly variable in the wild form, and it has become one of the best experimental animals for the fish geneticist. Because the various markings and color patterns can be directly correlated with specific hereditary factors (genes), it has been possible by systematic selection to produce a large number of domesticated forms which are radically different from the wild form in color and shape of fins. Certain forms have been developed which are highly ornamental. New types are still being produced, while others have disappeared. Certain aquarium clubs have specifically dedicated themselves to the perpetuation of various domesticated forms. Unfortunately, these artificial forms are often much more delicate than the wild ones. They require higher temperatures and are more susceptible to disease. There is, of course, the constant risk of degeneration due to continued inbreeding.

The two sexes can readily be distinguished. Males are smaller than females and also far more colorful. They can also be recognized—just as in all other livebearer males—by the presence of the gonopodium, the sex organ. Females are substantially larger but have rather plain coloration. Guppies will breed readily in any size tank, including a community tank. The young, released fully developed from the female, will tend to swim along the surface. Unfortunately guppies, just as all other livebearers, tend to pursue their own young and feed on them. So in order to protect baby fishes the tank has to be well planted, particularly with those plants with long, bushy leaves, thus affording the young sufficient hiding places.

The ideal water temperature should fall somewhere around 20° to 22°C (maximum range from 16° to 30°C), and the water should not be too soft (most livebearers prefer harder, slightly alkaline water). Guppies are not particularly selective as far as their food is concerned. Most dried foods (flakes) are readily accepted, but these should be supplemented periodically with other items such as tubifex worms, water fleas *(Daphnia),* cyclops, mosquito larvae, algae and occasionally some lettuce or spinach.

1 The development of brilliant colors and long fins in livebearers has enhanced their popularity in the aquarium hobby. Sometimes, however, long finnage causes problems in guppies (1) by inhibiting their swimming ability. Photo by H. Kyselov. (2) Long-finned swordtails often cannot reproduce without the aid of artificial insemination, because the length of the male's gonopodium (which is derived from the anal fin) makes the organ non-functional.

MOLLIES AND RELATED FORMS
(*Poecilia (Mollienesia)* spp.)

This is a small group of relatively large livebearers (up to about 15 cm for some females) which includes a couple of very attractive domesticated and/or hybridized forms. While they are easily kept and bred in captivity, it is difficult to obtain offspring that develop normally. These fishes feed on large amounts of herbivorous matter (plants) which are often difficult to supply in a home aquarium situation. Therefore, the most beautiful specimens are invariably those which have been bred in open ponds in the tropics (Florida). The following three forms are commonly available in the tropical fish trade because they are the most suitable ones in this group.

Black Molly

Black individuals are common in nature in all *Mollienesia* species, which have become totally intermixed, and they are commonly offered as black mollies in tropical fish stores. These fishes require a fair amount of heat, and thus water temperatures should never drop below 23 °C; the ideal range is 23° to 28 °C.

The females are substantially larger and heavier than males; the latter are recognized by the presence of the gonopodium. Since these fishes have a tendency to nibble on plants, these should be of the hardy type such as *Vallisneria* and other leafy plants. The tank should have some open swimming space. Black mollies, like the other *Mollienesia,* are very susceptible to sudden water changes. A newly set up aquarium should be left standing for a week or two before fish are introduced. If the fish show signs of discomfort (closed fins, lethargic movements) the addition of some salt (sodium chloride or sea salt) often improves their condition. The diet should be the same as described above for guppies.

Other Mollies

The three common species of *Mollienesia (Poecilia (M.) latipinna*—sailfin molly, *P.(M.) velifera*—Yucatan molly, and *P.(M.) sphenops*—Mexican molly) vary greatly in nature. Moreover, several domesticated forms have been developed from all three and these have been further hybridized, so that it is impossible in many cases to give these proper names. A spectacularly enlarged dorsal fin is found only in the Yucatan molly and the sailfin molly, but these two species resemble each other very closely. The Mexican molly never has an enlarged dorsal fin.

Another distinct black form is the so-called lyretail molly, which was developed in tropical fish hatcheries in Southeast Asia some years ago. It too is a popular aquarium fish, but it is not known from which *Mollienesia* species it was derived.

A good swordtail specimen has a long straight caudal fin extension or "sword" that has a black line along its lower edge. A small male having a long sword will not grow very much once the sword has become elongated. The male swordtail shown here has just about the right proportions. Photo by R. Zukal.

It is important for aquarists to remember that the different species of *Mollienesia* not be kept in the same tank since they all interbreed quite readily and the offspring are rarely as attractive as their parents.

SWORDTAILS

Another group of fishes within the livebearer family are the swordtails. Again, we are faced with a variety of domesticated and hybridized forms which are often difficult to distinguish from each other. The basic, wild form is the green swordtail, *Xiphophorus helleri*. It is an active schooling fish which does well in an aquarium. The females are again the larger animals in body; however, the smaller-bodied males have an elongated edge of the lower tail fin (the sword), which can give them a maximum length of about 15 cm. Several males kept in the same tank tend to be somewhat aggressive towards each other, although they will never attack other fishes.

Swordtails, too, breed easily and willingly in an aquarium, even in a community tank. However, precautions have to be taken to protect the young, which will otherwise be eaten quickly by their own parents. These fishes have no particular requirements as far as type of water, temperature and food are concerned.

The domesticated forms now commonly offered for sale in most larger tropical fish stores have different shades of red and green, and some have greatly enlarged dorsal fins.

PLATIES

Very similar in body form to swordtails are the platies, although they remain smaller and a sword is absent. The maximum size is about 4 cm to 7 cm. Most species occur in Central America, that is, the east coast of Mexico, southward to Honduras and beyond. Because of their small size and attractive colors they make excellent aquarium fishes. Indeed, platys are also among the most popular aquarium fishes. A number of domesticated forms have been developed and most of these arose from one of two original species: the platy (also called mirror platy), *Xiphophorus maculatus,* and the variable platy, *Xiphophorus variatus.* These two are very closely related. In the wild,

This platy shows the wild comet pattern in the tail. This is one of the hardiest strains of platies. Photo by R. Zukal.

The male platy on the left shows the wagtail color pattern (solid black fins) while the female (right) shows the "Mickey Mouse" pattern in the caudal peduncle. Both of these are well established strains that are fairly hardy aquarium fishes. Photo by R. Zukal.

both are highly variable in their markings and coloration, although there are some subtle anatomical differences which separate the two species.

All platies (including the domesticated forms) are very peaceful and thus ideal aquarium fishes. They are colorful and active and easily bred in virtually any size aquarium. As in most other livebearers, the female is larger than the male. The latter can be recognized, again, by the presence of the gonopodium. The female, which is often less colorful, has a distinct dark gravid spot in the area of the anal opening when young are about to be released.

There are no specific requirements other than a well-planted aquarium which still affords ample swimming space. The water temperature should not go beyond the extremes of 16° to 30°C, with 22° to 25°C being the most desirable temperature range. The food requirements are essentially the same as described above for the guppy.

There are a few other livebearing fishes belonging to a couple of other families. However, their care is somewhat more complicated and, therefore, they are not too often available from tropical fish stores. Moreover, they are not particularly well suited for the beginning aquarist.

The photo on the left shows a pair of checker barbs *(Capoeta oligolepis)* in a typical spawning position, with the tail of the male flung over the back of the female. Photo by R. Zukal. The red-tailed black shark, *Labeo bicolor,* is a popular cyprinid, but it may tend to harass smaller fishes in the aquarium. Photo by G. Senfft.

Egglayers

CARP-LIKE FISHES
(FAMILY CYPRINIDAE)

This family contains about 1,500 species which are most commonly found in either slow-moving or standing bodies of fresh water. Their distribution extends throughout Europe, Asia, Africa and North America. Many of the tropical and subtropical forms are small and colorful, attributes which make them ideal aquarium fishes. Most of the species commonly kept in home aquaria are not particularly demanding as far as their food requirements are concerned, although a few species require fairly soft water if they are to breed. Most of the other species will readily breed in just about any kind of reasonable water condition.

One of the most commonly kept carp-like fishes is indeed a carp, or rather, a very close relative . . . the goldfish and its many domesticated forms. Details as to how to keep these are available from numerous other publications available from most larger pet shops. Since this book is confined to discussing the tropical forms of this family, let us first take a look at some of the common barbs which have been aquarium "evergreens" since the early days of the tropical fish hobby.

The Barbs

This is a group with a large number of species, most of which occur in Africa and Asia. In fact, most of the more popular aquarium barbs come from Asia, or more specifically from the Indian subcontinent and from the islands of the Indo-Australian Archipelago.

There has been much confusion in recent years about the scientific name of these fishes. Essentially they are divided on the basis of the number of barbels present on the mouth (either none, two or four). For our purposes here the generic name *Puntius* is being retained, although the generic names *Capoeta* and *Barbodes* are often used interchangeably.

Undoubtedly, the most popular fish in this group is the tiger or Sumatra barb, *Puntius tetrazona*. It is a magnificently colored, very active schooling fish which has a "social pecking order" in each school. This fish requires a slightly larger tank (15 to 20 gallons and upward) if it is to be effectively displayed as a school. It is a very hardy fish which feeds eagerly on a wide variety of food items (dried foods and live foods). Unfortunately, the tiger barb has sometimes the nasty habit of nibbling on the fins of other tank occupants, particularly those which have fins ending in thin threads (angelfish, etc.). It grows to about 7 cm. The females can be recognized (in adult specimens) by their heavier, more robust body, and males have more intense colors (particularly the red and black). This fish requires a lot of swimming space, so the aquarium must not be too densely planted. It can be placed in a community tank with other species, but the barbs must be watched for their "nibbling" habit. The water temperature should be from 20° to 25°C and the water should be well aged, with occasional additions of new fresh water. The tiger barb occurs in Southeast Asia (Sumatra, Borneo, Thailand). In recent years a domesticated, albinistic (white) form has become very popular with aquarists. The requirements for it are the same as for the natural form.

Very similar to the tiger barb is the five-banded barb, *Puntius partipentazona,* which is characterized by the presence of an incomplete fifth vertical band extending partially down from the dorsal fin. It is somewhat more aggressive towards other fishes, particularly those which have long, extended fins. The requirements are essentially the same as for the previously discussed tiger barb, except this fish seems to be somewhat susceptible to sudden, large water changes. It accepts all kinds of available fish foods (dried and live); in fact, like all other barbs, it will do quite well on dried foods alone.

The calm, slow-moving parts of the mountain streams in Sri Lanka are inhabited by the black ruby barb, *Puntius nigrofasciatus,* which is also a very popular aquarium fish. It grows to about 6 cm in length. It is a hardy fish which does well in any community tank, provided ample swimming room is available. Barbels are not present alongside the mouth, and males can be recognized by their jet black dorsal fin. In fact, as in all other barbs, the males in this species are more colorful than the females, while the latter can be distinguished by their heavier, more robust body. The water should be well aged before they are introduced to the tank, and fresh water changes should be kept to a minimum. The ideal temperature range is from 20° to 28°C. The diet should be varied with occasional vegetable supplements (lettuce or spinach).

One of the classic aquarium fishes is the rosy barb, *Puntius conchonius*. It was previously very widespread and popular, but aquarists seem to prefer the more colorful tiger barb and its related forms, and so rosy barbs are nowadays less common in the tanks of tropical fish dealers. Normally this species is rather drab, silvery grayish in color, but at breeding time the male turns brilliant red. It is a very hardy fish and does well in just about any size tank (remember the maximum size is about 13 cm) and it is quite compatible with virtually all other fishes in a community tank. If anything detrimental can be said, then it is possibly the fact that rosy barbs tend to "dig" in accumulations of debris and other organic materials for food. However, in a tank properly kept clean this should not be a problem. Rosy barbs are quite tolerant to a wide variety of water conditions, as long as these do not exceed the already wide optimum temperature range from 17° to 25°C. This species occurs through wide areas of India.

Slightly smaller than the previously mentioned barbs is the golly barb, *Puntius oligolepis,* from Sumatra. Its maximum size will never exceed 5 cm. It is an active schooling fish, where the males tend to "spar" with each other without inflicting any serious injuries. Other than that it is a hardy, peaceful fish which does very well in any community tank. This species is characterized by the presence of a pair of barbels alongside the mouth. Adult males have an attractive reddish coloration and a distinctive black margin to the dorsal fin. The tank should be aged, with occasional additions of fresh water, and kept within a temperature range of from 20° to 25°C. The diet should be the same as mentioned above for the other barbs.

Similarly small is the cherry barb, *Puntius titteya,* from Sri Lanka. This is a somewhat shy fish which does best in a thickly planted tank, where it will often remain hidden if kept in single pairs or just as individual specimens. If a number of them are kept together they too will school—near the bottom—and remain fairly active. The water temperature should range from 23° to 26°C, and the diet should include regular vegetable supplements (algae or substitutes like lettuce or spinach). This species is characterized by a two-tone (gold/black) lateral band and the presence of a pair of barbels. The males are more colorful than the females, while the latter can be recognized by a heavier body and less intense colors.

The Rasboras

The genus *Rasbora* is widely distributed throughout the Indian subcontinent. It consists mainly of small, peaceful and often very colorful species which are among the most popular aquarium fishes. They are mainly schooling fishes that live in still or flowing waters, but some of the more colorful species live among dense vegetation in quiet pools. Unfortunately, some species are very difficult to keep or they are so small that they should not be placed in the type of community tank we are discussing here for the beginning aquarist. However, a few have become "aquarium staples" which also have a place in any community tank.

The most popular rasbora is the harlequin fish, *Rasbora heteromorpha,* from the Malay Peninsula, Thailand, Sumatra, Java and Borneo. It grows to a maximum size of about 4 cm. It is an active and very peaceful schooling fish which was once an expensive rarity in tropical fish stores. Now it is bred in enormous numbers in Southeast Asia (Hong Kong, Singapore), and so it has become available even to the beginning aquarist. However, it is somewhat specific in its requirements. The water should be slightly acid and soft, at a temperature of about 22° to 25°C. The tank should be planted fairly densely with fine, feathery plants but still leaving sufficient open swimming spaces. They are omnivorous fishes, feeding on a wide variety of items from dried foods to live water fleas, tubifex and similar items.

Another suitable fish for any community tank is the scissor-tail rasbora, *Rasbora trilineata,* from Sumatra and Borneo. This is a fairly large (for a *Rasbora;* 13 cm) but elegant fish which is very easy to keep. Its common name refers to characteristic "cutting" movements made by the tail. It is an active, schooling fish which tends to remain in the middle water region. This rasbora is an ideal community tank fish since it is peaceful and hardy. The water temperature should range from 18° to 25°C.

The redtail rasbora, *Rasbora borapetensis,* from Thailand is another peaceful and hardy community tank fish. It is an active schooling fish which requires ample swimming space. The aquarium should be well planted, but leave sufficient swimming room. The required water temperature is about 20° to 26°C. It should be noted here that virtually all rasboras prefer soft, slightly acid water, which can often be provided by filtering the water over peat moss (which must *not have* fertilizer additives).

The banded rasbora, *Rasbora einthoveni,* also makes a suitable community tank fish which should do well for the beginning aquarist. It is attractive, peaceful towards other fish and quite hardy. As an active fish it must have ample swimming space, thus planting should be confined to the periphery of the tank with an open space in the center. The water temperature should be from 22° to 25°C, with the water kept slightly on the soft and acid side. The diet, as for all rasboras, should be varied, but the fish is not demanding and will eagerly accept a staple diet of dried foods if nothing else is available. This species grows to about 8 cm and comes from Malayasia and some of the larger Indonesian islands.

Danios
This is a group of rather small barb-like fishes (genera *Danio* and *Brachydanio*) from Southeast Asia which are very popular with aquarists. Most species are very hardy

and peaceful and so they are ideal for the beginner. All of them can be kept in a community aquarium in the company of other fishes. However, the tank should be spacious, allowing for ample swimming space. The water should be slightly hard and a partial replacement of water should be made at regular intervals. The ideal temperature should fall within the range from 18° to 20°C, although these fishes can tolerate, for a short period of time, temperatures which fall slightly below that. If the water is suitable and the tank is kept in a sunny position most danios will spawn quite readily. However, for rearing the extremely small young special tanks and food will have to be provided. The eggs are deposited among the plants, and the parents must be removed immediately after spawning or they will eat their own eggs.

Except for some of the livebearing toothcarps, the zebra danio or zebrafish, *Brachydanio rerio,* is very much *the* beginner's fish. This is not to say that advanced aquarists cannot keep it, because a small school of these attractive, fast-moving fish will enhance the appearance of any aquarium. It is indeed a very robust and hardy fish which fits into even the smallest aquarium; its maximum size is 5 cm and it is characterized by two pairs of barbels. Females are slightly larger and fuller than males. The tank can be set up with plants as long as sufficient swimming room is being provided. Since zebrafish are, as indeed are most other danios, very rapid swimmers which tend to jump out of the tank, a proper, tight-fitting cover glass must be placed over the tank. This is a typical community tank fish which shows its full vitality and colors when exposed to some daily sunlight. Zebrafish are omnivorous, feeding on a wide variety of commercially available fish foods, live as well as dried.

Most danios come from Southeast Asia, while a number of them are restricted to the Indian subcontinent, especially to the eastern coast of India. The zebrafish is one of those species with a very narrow range of distribution.

Another very popular fish is the pearl danio, *Brachydanio albolineatus,* which comes from India, Burma, Thailand and the Malay Peninsula. It is an active but peaceful schooling fish which does well in even the smallest community tank. For the fullest appreciation of its colors and vitality this fish, like all other danios, should get sunlight every day. Again, males tend to remain slightly smaller than females and lack their full bodies. The tank MUST be covered tightly to prevent these fish from jumping out. Pearl danios are not quite as hardy as zebra danios, and so their water temperature should not fall below 20 °C. Most commercially available dried and live foods are eagerly eaten.

The spotted danio, *Brachydanio frankei,* is a more recent introduction to the tropical fish hobby, but it has already become very popular. It too is a very undemanding species which fits well into a community tank. Temperature and other requirements are the same as described for the previous two species.

Another active schooling fish is the Bengal danio, *Danio devario,* which prefers the upper regions of an aquarium. It is a peaceful and hardy species which grows to a maximum size of about 10 cm. The tank can be well planted provided sufficient open areas are left for this fish to display its full activity and colors. The females are less colorful but have a stouter, fuller body. This species is widely distributed over Southeast Asia. Like the other danios, it readily accepts all commercial foods.

The largest of the danios is the giant danio, *Danio malabaricus,* which grows to about 15 cm. Despite its size it too is a good community tank fish. However, it must be provided with a larger tank than can be used for the other danios. The giant danio is a true schooling fish that should never be kept alone or in single pairs. It prefers the upper water layers, close to the surface. Because of its size, this fish should be provided with lots of swimming space, and so the tank should only be planted along the sides and the back and have much open space in its center. Females are characterized by their heavier body, and the median blue line along the body bends slightly upwards close to the tail. In males this line remains straight over its entire length. The giant danio comes from the west coast of India and from Sri Lanka and should be given a water temperature of about 20° to 24°C. This fish is truly omnivorous, accepting virtually all commercially available live and dried foods.

Other Cyprinid Fishes

Apart from danios, rasboras and barbs there are a whole host of other cyprinid (carp-like) fishes which have been introduced to the aquarium hobby. Here now are a few more species which are suitable for the beginning aquarist.

One of the hardiest aquarium fishes is, without a doubt, the White Cloud Mountain minnow or simply White Cloud, *Tanichthys albonubes*. This little 6 cm long fish occurs in the province of Canton, China (in the canyons of the "White Cloud Mountains"), where it was first discovered in 1932 by the Chinese zoologist Lin.

This fish thrives best at somewhat lower temperatures, from 18° to 22°C. It is an active and very peaceful little fish which does well in any community tank, where it remains in the middle water layers. The tank should be well planted but still afford sufficient swimming space. When this fish is kept in single pairs, they tend to breed readily, and the parents will not molest the young, which can be reared in the breeding tank. The young are even more beautiful than the adults because of the presence of a prominent bright iridescent green lateral band. Later on this band dulls considerably, but even adult White Clouds are still very attractive little fish with their red patches in the dorsal, tail and to a lesser degree in their anal fin. There should be frequent partial water changes to keep this fish in good condition. As far as food is concerned it will feed on all commercially available dried and live foods, provided that these are small enough to be swallowed.

Another carp-like fish which is gaining increasing popularity is the firetail or red-tailed shark, *Labeo bicolor.* The name "shark" is indeed misleading because this fish bears absolutely no relationship to true sharks; instead it is one of the carp-like freshwater fishes. It is a very attractive bicolored fish which grows to a maximum size of 20 cm. It is a very hardy fish which often lives for many years in an aquarium, provided it gets the necessary care and attention. The tank must be planted fairly densely so that the fish can hide if it wants to. There it tends to establish territories which it often fiercely defends against other firetails. Therefore, it is prudent to have only one or two (a pair) specimens in each tank. The water should be somewhat soft and slightly acidic (filtration of the water over peat moss is very effective for this fish). In nature this fish feeds to a large extent on algae, and thus its diet should include plant matter (such as algae, lettuce, dandelions, etc.). Other than that it will take most commercially available dried and live fish foods. The water temperature should be about 22° to 26°C. Firetails come from Southeast Asia (Thailand, Malay Peninsula).

Another even more effective algae-eater is the flying fox, *Epalzeorhynchus kallopterus,* from Thailand and the Malay Peninsula. This fish grows to a length of about 14 cm. It is fairly inactive, spending most of its time on the bottom or against the aquarium glass, grazing on algae and bottom detritus. As such it is very effective, and each aquarium should have at least one specimen as a "vacuum cleaner." It is a peaceful and very hardy little fish which prefers a water temperature of about 22° to 24°C. Other than algae it will also feed on various dried and live foods, but algae (or substitutes like lettuce or spinach) must be included in its diet.

LOACHES AND SPINY LOACHES
(FAMILY COBITIDAE)

The 80 or so members of this family are somewhat related to the carp-like fishes (Cyprinidae) just discussed. They are distributed throughout the "Old World," that is, from Spain across the whole of Eurasia to the Pacific coast. This includes the northern regions of Europe and Asia, and to the south their distribution extends locally into Africa (Morocco and Ethiopia). The loaches and spiny loaches attain their greatest diversity in southern Asia and the Malay Archipelago, and that is where most of the species come from which are now very popular aquarium fishes.

The common name "spiny loach" refers to a spine situated obliquely below and in front of the eye. The fish can erect this spine, which then can become fatal to any predator which preys upon the loach. Larger fishes and even birds often perish after swallowing loaches whose spines stick in their gullets.

The mouth is almost underneath the head and is surrounded by four or more pairs of barbels, of which at least one pair is situated on the snout. Certain species are able to utilize intestinal respiration, which enables many loaches to live in muddy, oxygen-depleted waters. These fishes rise to the surface and take in atmospheric air through the mouth; this is then passed into the intestine where oxygen is absorbed and waste carbon dioxide given off. The air is then expelled through the vent. Some loaches respond quite dramatically to variations in air pressure and become restless when this falls (a "live barometer").

The clear adaptation of loaches to a bottom-living habit is really betrayed by their shape, which is essentially worm-like in many forms. Loaches from mountain and lowland streams are mostly round or slightly flattened *(Noemacheilus)* in cross-section. Those from standing or slow-moving waters are compressed from side to side

(Botia, Acanthophthalmus). Many loaches, at times, burrow into sand or mud.

Those species commonly available and which are suitable for the community tank of a beginning aquarist include the following:

Coolie loach, *Acanthophthalmus kuhlii;* Indonesia; 7.5 cm;

Half-banded loach, *Acanthophthalmus semicinctus;* Sunda Islands; 7.5 cm;

Slimy loach, *Acanthophthalmus myersi;* S.E. Thailand; 7.5 cm;

Clown loach, *Botia macracanthus;* Sunda Islands; 30 cm;

Orange-finned loach, *Botia modesta;* S.E. Asia; 10 cm;

Banded loach, *Botia hymenophysa;* Malaysia, Sunda Islands; 30 cm;

Dwarf loach, *Botia sidthimunki;* Thailand; 4 cm.

Most loaches and spiny loaches are extremely hardy fishes, but in an aquarium situation special consideration must be given to the shy and retiring nature of these fishes. Their well-being depends very much on the lighting situation and on the availability of suitable hiding places. The tank should be fairly dark. Plants can be very sparse as long as there are ample hiding places (inverted coconut shells, flower pot fragments, etc.) and the bottom consists of fine sand (in which some loaches like to burrow).

Although single specimens can be kept together with other fishes in a community tank, loaches are most effective when they are kept in small groups and by themselves. Soft to medium hard water, which is partially replaced at frequent intervals, is quite adequate for keeping loaches. The water temperature should be 25° to 30°C, and, especially at the higher temperature, the tank should be well aerated, since many species require a large amount of oxygen.

In the wild the food of loaches consists primarily of worms and insect larvae obtained while they "scour" around the debris on the bottom. Some species eat plant material, mainly in the form of algae. In captivity they will take various live foods (daphnia, cyclops, enchytraeid worms, mosquito larvae) as well as dried foods. Some species must have vegetable matter in the form of algae or substitutes like lettuce, spinach, rolled oats, etc.

CHARACINS OR TETRAS
(FAMILY CHARACIDAE)

This is a very diverse family of fishes. It has several sub-families and is characterized by great species, form and color diversity. As a group, the characins contribute the greatest number of species to the aquarium hobby, and some of the most popular aquarium fishes are among them. Most characins are very good aquarium fishes; they are invariably hardy, peaceful and many are extremely colorful. Nevertheless, among their close relatives are some rather infamous predators such as piranhas and a few others.

Characins (or tetras as they are more commonly called in the aquarium trade) are distributed throughout southern North America, Central America, South America and a few occur in Africa. Most species have behind the dorsal fin a small rayless fat—or adipose—fin.

Tetras must have clear and clean water; but their oxygen needs are not too strict. However, few species will breed in a community aquarium since they have exceedingly high demands for clean water when breeding. Their eggs are extremely susceptible to fungal and bacterial attacks, which invariably go hand-in-hand with dirty water. Breeding requirements are sometimes quite specific, the details of which are beyond the scope of this little book.

Neon and Cardinal Tetras

The most popular fish in this group is, without a doubt, the spectacular neon tetra, *Paracheirodon innesi*, from the dark, acidic waters of the upper reaches of the Amazon River in South America. Its maxium size is about 4 cm. It is one of the most beautiful aquarium fishes and—to the advantage of the beginning hobbyist—it is also very hardy. As a typical schooling fish it prefers the company of a number of its mates. The tank should be planted densely, and the bottom should be dark, so that the iridescent colors of the neon tetras are most effectively shown. This effect can be enhanced further by using the so-called "Gro-Lux" fluorescent light tubes, which emphasize the colors even more.

The neon tetra is very hardy, thriving in almost any kind of water as long as the temperature is in the range of 20° to 25°C. However, ideally the water should be soft and slightly acid, something which can easily be achieved by filtering the water over peat moss. Neon tetras will respond by showing even more brilliant colors. Water changes should be kept to a minimum. This fish does well on a variety of foods, dried or live.

In contrast to its hardiness in a community tank, it is very difficult to breed, a fact which contributed for many years to excessively high prices. Once it became clear that the fish has specific water requirements for breeding and once these were established, it was bred prolifically in captivity.

For years the neon tetra was the "jewel" among the aquarium fishes. Therefore, the introduction in 1956 of another neon-type fish with even more spectacular coloration (than the neon tetra) created quite a sensation. This was the cardinal tetra, *Cheirodon axelrodi*. This 4 cm long fish originates from a tributary of the Amazon (Rio Negro) in South America. It is generally a hardy and very peaceful fish which does well in the community tank of a beginning aquarist. The tank should be well planted but still have ample open swimming space, with a water temperature of about 23° to 25°C. Water changes should be kept to a minimum; ideally the water should be soft and slightly acid (peat filtration). Cardinal tetras are not demanding as far as their food is concerned; they will feed on nearly all commercially available dried and live foods.

In addition to these two "jewels" among tetras, in fact among all aquarium fishes, there are a whole host of other, often very attractively colored characins which are "staples" of the aquarium fish business. Many of these are excellent as fishes for beginning aquarists, but there are too many to be mentioned here in detail. Most of these fall into the two genera *Hyphessobrycon* and *Hemigrammus*, and their basic requirements as far as water chemistry, temperature and diet are concerned are largely similar, if not outright identical. Thus, only a few examples are given on the following pages.

Genus *Hyphessobrycon*

One of the earliest imported tetras, and also a very attractive one, is the flame tetra, *Hyphessobrycon flammeus*, from Rio de Janeiro. Its maximum size is about 4.5 cm. This is a very hardy and peaceful fish that should not be absent from any beginner's aquarium. It is a schooling fish, and several specimens will form an attractive school which tends to swim in the middle or lower region of the tank. The females are larger and more robust, but lack the brighter colors (red) and the black margin in the anal fin of males. The tank should be well planted but still provide ample swimming room. Flame tetras are excellent community tank fish which readily accept most available foods. The most suitable water temperature range is 20° to 25 °C, and water changes should be kept to a minimum.

Another attractive group of tetras are the so-called "rosy tetras." This involves a group of several species of tetras which all look superficially rather similar. Characteristically, they have a base coloration of red with various amounts of black as margins on the dorsal and anal fins. Some have a dark or red "shoulder spot" and bright reds in their tail. Essentially, these species include the rosy tetra, *Hyphessobrycon bentosi*, the jewel tetra, *Hyphessobrycon callistus*, and serpae tetras, *Hyphessobrycon serpae* (several subspecies). The largest of the "rosy tetra" group is the bleeding heart tetra, *Hyphessobrycon erythrostigma*, which is characterized by a blood-red spot on the flank.

All of these tetras are very attractive schooling fishes which should never be kept alone. They tend to form loosely-knit schools which stay in the lower water region. The tank should always be well planted but there must be ample swimming room. Some of them (e.g., *H. bentosi*) have a tendency to form some sort of territory which leads to mild aggression towards other rosy tetras, but by-and-large these fishes are rather peaceful. If given an adequate water temperature of 22° to 26°C, with water changes kept to a minimum, they do well in any community tank. The maximum size (e.g., bleeding heart tetra) is 8 cm, but most of them grow only to about 5 or 6 cm. Most of these fishes occur in central South America, mainly in the Amazon and its tributaries. The males are invariably distinguished by their more intense (red) coloration and distinct black markings in the dorsal and along the margin of the anal fin. The diet should consist of a variety of high quality dried foods and certain live foods.

Another group of *Hyphessobrycon* tetras are characterized by a distinct black lateral line along the side of the body, often ending in a red or reddish tail. One of the most conspicuous members in this group is the hardy black neon, *Hyphessobrycon herbertaxelrodi*. This little (4.5 cm) fish comes from the upper regions of the Amazon (Mato Grosso, Rio Taquary). It is an active but peaceful schooling fish which likes densely planted tanks with ample swimming room. The water temperature should be fairly warm (24° to 26°C), with minimum water changes. Black neon tetras are essentially omnivorous, feeding on most commercially available foods, but they should have occasional vegetable supplements (algae, lettuce, etc.).

The lemon tetra, *Hyphessobrycon pulchripinnis*, also has been a very popular tetra for many years, and it is certainly one of the ideal fishes for the beginning aquarist. Like other tetras it too is an active, schooling fish which tends to congregate in certain areas of the tank, which should be well planted. It is a peaceful fish which can be kept together with many other species in a community tank. The water should ideally be slightly acid, although this fish is not too particular about water conditions. Its dietary requirements are the same as those described for the other tetras.

Genus *Hemigrammus*

The genus *Hemigrammus* contains a number of tetras which have been favorites among aquarists for many years. The most popular (and by far the most attractive) one is the glowlight tetra, *Hemigrammus erythrozonus* (which was formerly known erroneously as *Hyphessobrycon gracilis*). It is a hardy fish which should be kept in soft, moderately acid water at a temperature of 23° to 28°C. Although this tetra also forms little schools when a number of them are being kept together, it has a tendency to establish a territory which it defends against intruders of its own kind. Females are distinguished by their stouter bodies and slightly larger size. The tank should be well planted but retain a fair amount of open swimming space. Glowlight tetras are good community tank fish which look particularly attractive when kept together with neon and cardinal tetras. This species occurs in northeastern South America (Guyana), where it lives in slow-moving streams.

Somewhat different in appearance is the pretty tetra, *Hemigrammus pulcher,* with its characteristically high body shape. It is a very quiet schooling fish which tends to prefer the lower water regions, forming a certain territory. The maximum size of this fish is about 6 cm, and it prefers fairly warm water (25° to 28°C). Females are larger than males, and the anal fin in males is white at its origin. This fish comes from the upper and middle regions of the Amazon in South America. Like other tetras it feeds on a variety of foods, and it can even subsist on a total diet of some of the better dried foods.

The head-and-tail light tetra, *Hemigrammus ocellifer,* is another aquarium fish from South America which has been around for many years. It still enjoys considerable popularity, simply because it is an attractive and hardy fish which does well in almost any community aquarium. Its maximum size is about 4.5 cm, and it should be kept at temperatures ranging from 22° to 27°C. Water changes should be kept to a minimum, because it sometimes shows a slight susceptibility to the addition of large amounts of fresh water. Females are heavier and more robust than males. It has been hypothesized that the bright markings (i.e., the "head and tail lights") are supposed to guide straying members of the school back to the main group when they have become lost in dark pools in the rain forest, where little light penetrates.

Also very characteristically colored is the red-nosed or rummy-nosed tetra, *Hemigrammus rhodostomus,* which can easily be recognized by its red face and mouth region. This is a very attractive schooling fish which is hardy and peaceful. It does very well, indeed, in a community tank. Females are larger with a stouter body than males. The latter have a tiny hook on the anal fin, which often causes them to get "hung up" in nets when they are being transferred. The tank should be densely planted but still have plenty of open, unobstructed swimming space. The ideal water temperature is between 23° to 25°C. Contrary to most other tetras, rummy-nosed tetras should have frequent partial water changes, which seems to be indicative of its origin in the lower reaches of the Amazon River where there are constant water changes from the incoming tributaries. Like other tetras, this one too feeds on a variety of commercially available dried and live foods.

Apart from the main groups (genera) of tetras (i.e., *Hyphessobrycon* and *Hemigrammus*) there are also a large number of other characins which make excellent aquarium fishes, particularly for the beginning aquarist. A few of these, that is, the more common and readily available ones,should now be mentioned to round off the picture of species diversity, which is so typical for this large family of fishes.

Other Tetras

A rather unique characin which is easily kept by the beginning aquarist is the blind cave fish, *Astyanax fasciatus mexicanus ("Anoptichthys jordani")*. It is a small fish (6.5 cm), which occurs in subterranean limestone caves and water courses in Mexico, where it lives in total darkness. It is blind and unpigmented, but its lateral line is so well developed that it can detect minute changes in pressure and thus orientate itself nearly as well as sighted fish. The blind cave fish is very active, hardy and peaceful, and does well in an aquarium when kept under proper conditions. The tank should resemble a dark cave with little direct light, just enough to keep some of those plants which require not too much light. Therefore, this fish is best kept by itself (in what is known as a *species display*), possibly together with some catfishes (to be discussed later on). The water requirements are for relatively hard water, slightly on the alkaline side (frequent partial water changes and replacements recommended). The water temperature should be about 26° to 29 °C (fairly warm). This fish feeds readily on all commercially available foods.

Another "regular" among aquarium fishes is the diamond tetra, *Moenkhausia pittieri*, a 6 cm-long fish from Venezuela. It is a very distinctive fish with a longish, extended dorsal fin and shining scales. It is an active schooling fish which occupies the middle to upper water layers in an aquarium. This tetra does well in a community tank. The water should be soft and slightly acid, at a temperature from 22° to 26 °C. Although it is an active fish, the tank should be planted fairly well, but still provide sufficient open space as swimming room. The food requirements are essentially the same as for the previously discussed species.

More conspicuous because of its shape than its coloration is the black tetra, *Gymnocorymbus ternetzi*. It is a rather high-bodied fish with a somewhat ventrally extended abdominal cavity, which is pointed in males and rounded in females. The body from the level of the dorsal fin backward is jet black (including the anal fin), and there are two vertical black bars on the anterior half of the fish. Unfortunately, this black coloration fades with age so that young specimens are invariably more attractive than fully grown adults. It is a territorial but still very peaceful fish which can be kept even in very small aquariums. Its maximum size is about 6 cm. The black tetra is not particular when it comes to water quality, although it seems to prefer slightly harder water (than other tetras). Water changes should be kept to a minimum. The preferred temperature range is about 23° to 25°C. The food requirements are essentially the same as those for the previously discussed tetras.

Another "regular" has been, for many years, the X-ray tetra or simply pristella, *Pristella maxillaris*. This 5.5 cm long fish has its name derived from the fact that its abdominal cavity is partially transparent, showing some of the internal organs quite clearly. In males this cavity is pointed, while in females it is rounded off. Like the other tetras, it too is an active fish which is peaceful and quite hardy in any community tank. The tank should not be illuminated too brightly and should have a dark bottom. This presents the fish in its most favorable coloration and behavior. The pristella occurs throughout northern South America (Venezuela, Guyana).

From the lower Rio La Plata, around Ozario, in Argentina, comes the 5.5. cm long bloodfin, *Aphyocharax anisitsi*. It is an active and undemanding schooling fish which is very suitable for beginning aquarists. The tank should have dense peripheral plant growth with plenty of swimming room, although this species tends to stay in the middle to upper water layers. The preferred temperature range is 17° to 28°C, with no particular water requirements.

The penguin tetra or just penguin, *Thayeria boehlkei*, is another very characteristic species, primarily because of the way it maintains its position in the water: it is always in a slightly oblique position. With its head higher than its tail it appears to be standing on its tail . . . like a penguin. Despite its unique (for tetras) swimming position it is an active, schooling fish which is hardy and does well in an aquarium, even for beginning aquarists. There has been some confusion about the scientific name of this species; for many years it has been confused with another species, *T. obliqua*, and, unfortunately, this name still persists in some areas and among "old timer" aquarists. Water and food requirements are the same as those discussed for the other tetras.

Another very stunning tetra is the emperor tetra, *Nematobrycon palmeri*, a 5.5 cm long fish from the west slope of the Colombian Andes Mountains. Unlike most other tetras this is not truly a schooling fish. Nevertheless, it is hardy and most attractive, with its extended dorsal, anal and tail fins in adult specimens, and with its black lateral band and the iridescent bluish sheen on the upper back and head. Males often go through extensive "sparring" without ever seriously hurting each other. The water should ideally be soft and acid, although the emperor tetra usually does well under almost all conditions commonly found in a community tank.

PENCILFISHES (FAMILY LEBIASINIDAE)

These fishes were originally included in the family Characidae but have now been separated from them because of their toothless lower jaw.

Pencilfishes, exclusively native to Central and northern

South America, are, because of their small size and attractive coloration, very popular aquarium fishes. In the wild they inhabit small, flowing, weedy or shaded waters of a soft and slightly acid type, rather like the dark water of a peat bog. Many species are fishes of the surface layers, where they search for insects, their primary food. This is reflected in a special adaption seen in some pencilfishes. These take up an oblique position in which they swim quietly with their head pointing towards the surface *(Nannostomus eques)*.

Pencilfishes commonly available from tropical fish stores are:

Dwarf pencilfish, *Nannostomus marginatus;* Surinam; 4 cm;

Three-lined pencilfish, *Nannostomus trifasciatus;* Middle Amazon; 6 cm;

Tube-mouthed pencilfish, *Nannostomus eques;* Middle Amazon; 5 cm;

Beckford's pencilfish, *Nannostomus beckfordi;* Guianas, lower Rio Negro, lower and middle Amazon basin; 5 cm.

All pencilfishes should be kept in densely planted tanks, which can be either small or large. The water should be soft and acidic (very important), and water changes should be kept to a minimum. The ideal temperature range is 25° to 28 °C. The diet should be varied, but because of the small sized mouth size in these fishes the food must be correspondingly small (ideally small live food such as daphnia, etc.).

HATCHETFISHES (FAMILY GASTEROPELECIDAE

Hatchetfishes form a small characteristic family, widely distributed in South America. The deep body shape ("hatchet") is the result of a peculiar enlargement of the shoulder girdle. This causes the protrusion of the breast region, which resembles that of a bird. It is used as anchorage for the large muscles of the pectoral fins. This gives these fishes the power and ability to virtually "shoot" out of the water and glide for distances of up to 5 m over the surface. Because of their peculiar appearance and peacefulness hatchetfishes have become popular aquarium fishes. The following are commonly available:

Marbled hatchetfish, *Carnegiella strigata;* Amazon basin; 3.5 cm;

Silver hatchetfish, *Gasteropelecus levis;* Lower Amazon; 6 cm;

Common hatchetfish, *Gasteropelecus sternicla;* Amazon region; 6.5 cm.

Hatchetfishes are best kept in long, *well-covered* tanks, with a dark bottom and soft, slightly acid water. They are typical surface fishes, so plants are not particularly important, although these fishes like to congregate around hanging root systems and the broad leaves of floating plants. The temperature should be 23° to 30°C. Live food is fairly important for hatchetfishes; ideally they should be offered mosquito larvae, daphnia, vinegar flies, fruit flies, etc. Sometimes dried food is also eagerly taken. Hatchetfishes can be kept in community tanks together with other peaceful fishes, such as tetras, for instance.

MAILED OR ARMORED CATFISHES
(FAMILY CALLICHTHYIDAE)

Most of the catfishes—or "scavengers" as they are often called among aquarists—belong to this family, which has representatives throughout South America. Very characteristic for the whole family are the bony plates (armor) on the flanks, arranged in two series, overlapping like tiles on a roof. The head and the ridge of the back may also be armored, and the tiny adipose fin has a strong movable spine.

Most of these catfishes live in slowly flowing waters. Usually they form small groups in search of anything edible in shallow water. On occasions they also investigate mud and sandbanks. The powerful pectoral fin spines are used like "stilts" when these fishes are moving about on land. The respiration of these catfishes is also well adapted to an almost amphibious way of life. When outside of water (i.e., on a mud bank) or when the stagnant water in which they sometimes live has become foul with little oxygen left, the hind-gut can act as an air-breathing organ.

Almost all mailed catfishes are quite hardy and they adapt well to a life in captivity. Their often inquisitive, almost tame behavior has made them favorites with many aquarists and they are indeed immensely popular in the hobby. In addition to their quaint behavior, they are also very useful members in any community tank, since they clean up left-over food and other organic debris. These fishes constantly scour through the mulm on the bottom in search of something edible (thus "scavengers"). However, if food is in short supply, that is, there is no mulm on the bottom of the tank, mailed catfishes will quickly lose condition. Then, in desperate search of food they begin to dig into the bottom substrate, which can cause considerable annoyance to the aquarists who like to have a neat and clean tank. In any event, if a number of catfishes are being kept, an efficient filtration system must be installed. Large numbers of catfishes should be kept by themselves in a separate tank; however, a few individuals are a useful addition to any community tank.

By-and-large catfishes are very peaceful. They have a wide temperature tolerance (19° to 26°C), and they place no special demands on the water chemistry. Water changes can be kept to a minimum. They are truly omnivorous, feeding on all sorts of organic matter. All commercially available dried and live foods are eagerly eaten.

Although this family includes a number of different groups (genera), the largest number of individuals commonly available from tropical fish stores belong to the genus *Corydoras*. These are short, stout fishes with a relatively high, arched back. They range in size from 3 cm to about 10 cm, with the majority of species being around 5 to 7 cm as their maximum length.

Although none of the 20 or so commonly available species are spectacularly colored, many of them have rather conspicuous dark, sometimes black, markings, as dots, lines, bands or dark mottled patterns.

Since the various *Corydoras* species are virtually identical in regard to their biology and aquarium requirements, only a short list of the more frequently available species is given below:

Bronze corydoras, *Corydoras aeneus,* size to 7 cm;

Arched corydoras, *Corydoras arcuatus,* size to 6.5 cm;

Banded corydoras, *Corydoras barbatus,* size to 10 cm;

Elegant corydoras, *Corydoras elegans,* size to 6 cm;

Leopard corydoras, *Corydoras julii,* size to 6 cm;

Black-spotted corydoras, *Corydoras melanistius,* size to 6 cm;

Myers' corydoras, *Corydoras myersi,* size to 6 cm;

Peppered corydoras, *Corydoras paleatus,* size to 7 cm;

Spotted corydoras, *Corydoras punctatus,* size to 6 cm;

Dwarf corydoras, *Corydoras rabauti,* size to 3 cm;

Reticulated corydoras, *Corydoras reticulatus,* size to 7 cm.

SUCKERMOUTH CATFISHES
(FAMILY LORICARIIDAE)

This is another group of catfishes which are not only interesting but also quite useful for the home aquarium. They are confined to northern and central South America, where they inhabit mainly small and very rapidly flowing streams, although some members are also found towards the mouths of rivers, that is, in a slightly brackish water. Typical for these catfishes is a strong bony armor on the body, which is somewhat reminiscent of that found in the previously discussed mailed catfishes (family Callichthyidae), but there are significant differences. However, most characteristic for these fishes is a ventral mouth surrounded by broad, lobed lips. It serves as a sucking-mouth which represents a notable adaptation to the natural environment of the fish. The Loricariidae are bottom-dwellers which live among stones or roots and work themselves forward by clinging to these objects to brace themselves against the forces of sometimes strong currents. They are able to swim in midwater only for short periods of time. Their food consists primarily of algae which are grazed off stones, rocks, submerged branches and trees and plants.

Almost all of the suckermouth catfishes can be kept in aquaria, certainly as small specimens, although a couple eventually become quite large. In fact, many species, like members of *Otocinclus* and *Hypostomus*, are often very useful in any aquarium, since they keep down algal growth by grazing it off plants, stones and aquarium walls in a short period of time, with the added advantage that the plants are not being damaged.

All species are quite hardy as far as water conditions are concerned. The required temperature range is 20° to 25 °C, and temporary cooling down seems to do no harm. The larger species of *Hypostomus* and *Xenocara* can be kept only in large tanks. However, it must be noted here that even these "giants" are totally harmless and will not attack small fishes.

All suckermouth catfishes are more or less nocturnal and thus they like to hide during the day, either behind stones and plants or simply buried in sand (which should be fine-grained and soft).

Although they feed on a variety of foods (dried and live) their principal food should be algae, supplemented by lettuce leaves, spinach, etc.

Since the various suckermouth catfishes are virtually identical in regard to their aquarium requirements, only a short list of the more frequently available species is given below:

Ancistrus cirrhosus; Paraguay, Amazon Basin, Guyana; size to 14 cm;

Farlowella acus; Venezuela, Brazil; size to 14.5 cm; (three different *Farlowella* species have so far been imported);

Hypostomus plecostomus; La Plata region; size to 61 cm;

Loricaria filamentosa; Amazon; size to 25 cm;

Loricaria lanceolata; Amazon; size to 13 cm;

Loricaria parva; Paraguay and La Plata; size to 12 cm;

Otocinclus affinis; southeastern Brazil; size to 4 cm;

Plecostomus commersoni; La Plata Basin; size to 40 cm;

Xenocara multispinis; Humboldt River, Novo River; size to 12 cm.

CICHLIDS (FAMILY CICHLIDAE)

This is a large family of fishes containing several hundred species distributed throughout tropical South America, Central America, Africa and two species in India. Many of them are very attractively colored fishes of sunfish-like appearance, although certain features separate them from the sunfishes.

In their natural habitat cichlids occur in standing or slow-moving waters where there are good hiding places under banks, water-logged branches and trees, behind stones or in water plant thickets. Many species are highly territorial, defending their area against any and all intruders. Apart from a few species which feed almost exclusively on plants, most cichlids are aggressive predators feeding on smaller fishes (even their own species) and upon a variety of aquatic invertebrates (insect larvae, water beetles, worms, etc.).

Many cichlids are spectacularly colored, especially during the breeding season, but it is their predatory, highly aggressive behavior which makes most of them totally unsuitable for a community tank. In fact, the largest majority should be kept in their own tank, which then assures successful breeding, which is really the principal objective for most aquarists who keep these interesting but somewhat rambunctious fishes.

Below only those cichlids which can safely be kept in a

community tank are going to be discussed. The prime factor for selecting these is *size*. Traditionally, aquarists have divided cichlids into "regulars" and "dwarf cichlids." This is a purely arbitrary division which restricts the usage of "dwarf cichlids" primarily to the genus *Apistogramma* and to a few other species. All-in-all, this includes about 10 species or so which are commonly available, but only a few should be mentioned here.

The most common cichlid in home aquariums today is the angelfish or scalare, *Pterophyllum scalare*. It occurs over a wide geographical range in South America, and thus several variations are known. It is the most conspicuous one of all the cichlids because of its striking appearance as a high-bodied fish with long, extended dorsal and anal fins and three vertical dark bands (one going through the eye) set off against a silvery body color. The maximum size is up to 15 cm long and 25 cm high (tip of dorsal fin to tip of anal fin).

The angelfish is a quiet, peaceful schooling fish which does best when kept in a tank by itself together with several of its mates. Nevertheless, it will also do well in a community tank, provided other tank inmates do not harass it. For instance, some of the barbs have a tendency to "nibble" on the extended fins and fin threads, severely affecting the appearance of these strikingly beautiful fish.

The angelfish is not particular about temperature (22° to 30° C) or type of water, but it may be rather fastidious about food; it prefers a variety of live foods, such as daphnia, tubifex, mosquito larvae, etc. Large specimens will also eagerly take small guppies and very small tetras (neon and cardinal tetras preferred), thus the aquarist has to be careful. The tank should be well planted with tall, leafy plants such as *Vallisneria*, *Echinodorus* and others but still afford ample swimming space.

In recent years a number of color and fin mutations have been developed commercially, some of which are rather

THE WORLD'S LARGEST SELECTION OF PET, ANIMAL, AND MUSIC BOOKS.

T.F.H. Publications publishes more than 900 books covering many hobby aspects (dogs, cats, birds, fish, small animals, music, etc.). Whether you are a beginner or an advanced hobbyist you will find exactly what you're looking for among our complete listing of books. For a free catalog fill out the form on the other side of this page and mail it today.

. . CATS . . .

. . . BIRDS . .

. . . ANIMALS . . .

. . . DOGS . . .

. . FISH . . .

. . . MUSIC . . .

grotesque and bear no resemblance to the most attractive wild form of this species.

The most attractive of the smaller, so-called dwarf cichlids is the ram or butterfly cichlid, *Apistogramma ramirezi*. This pretty fish is sometimes called *Microgeophagus* or *Papiliochromis ramirezi*. This little, 5 cm long "jewel" of a fish originates from Venezuela, and it caused quite a sensation when it first appeared on the tropical fish market. Its coloration is indeed stunning and it is a very peaceful fish which prefers to remain close to the bottom. Unfortunately, it lives only for about two years or so, but it can be bred even in a small aquarium quite successfully. The sexes are somewhat difficult to distinguish, although the male has longer, extended fins (dorsal and anal), while females ready to spawn often have a redder abdominal area.

The tank should be densely planted and offer adequate hiding places (stones, water-logged driftwood, etc.), but there must also be ample swimming room. This fish is quite suitable for a community tank. The water temperature should be about 22° to 26° C, with reasonably soft water. This fish prefers frequent partial changes of water, which should be filtered over peat moss to give it some slight acidity. Like most other cichlids it is primarily carnivorous, feeding on water fleas, cyclops, tubifex and small mosquito larvae. Sometimes it will also accept dried foods.

In recent years a golden mutation of this species has appeared on the market. While it is also a very attractive fish, it lacks the spectacularly contrasting colors of the wild form. It too is quite suitable for a community tank.

Another attractive, small cichlid is Agassiz' dwarf cichlid, *Apistogramma agassizi*. It is a peaceful fish which does well in a community tank. It is characterized by a long, drawn-out tail in males (rounded off in females) and attains a maximum size of about 8 cm. The aquarium should afford suitable hiding places but also have ample open swimming

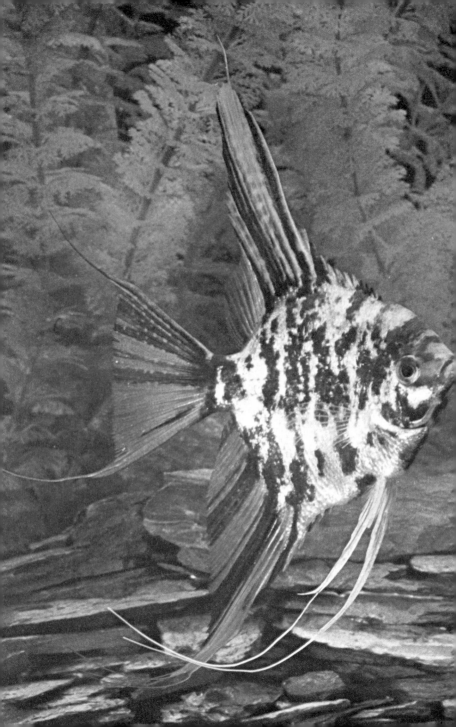

(1) Angelfish, *Pterophyllum scalare,* are available in a number of different color varieties including this marbled strain. Photo courtesy of Wardley Products Co. (2) *Apistogramma ramirezi* is an extremely colorful and peaceful dwarf cichlid species. Photo by R. Zukal. (3) *Apistogramma agassizi* is one of the few dwarf cichlids having a spear-shaped caudal fin. Photo by H.J. Richter.

space. The water temperature should be 19° to 25° C (the upper end of this range is required for breeding), and the water must be soft and slightly acid (peat moss filtration). Frequent partial water changes are recommended. The food is the same as that for *A. ramirezi,* mentioned above.

One of the earliest imported dwarf cichlids is the yellow dwarf cichlid, *Apistogramma reitzigi.* It is an attractive, yellow-colored cichlid which is peaceful and does well in a community tank, where it tends to occupy the lower water layers, remaining close to the plant cover. There should also be small rocks, pieces of water-logged driftwood and other potential hiding places. The maximum size of this fish is about 8 cm; it originates from the Rio Paraguay in South America. Males are characterized by a tall, sail-like dorsal fin; females remain smaller than males. The water should be soft and slightly acid; frequent partial water changes are recommended. Food as in *A. ramirezi,* discussed above.

The spotted dwarf cichlid, *Apistogramma ornatipinnis,* is another cichlid which does well in a community tank. It forms territories among plants and stones, usually in the back of the aquarium, but it is not excessively aggressive towards other fishes. This fish comes originally from western Guyana, northern South America, and grows to a maximum size of about 7 cm. It requires some hiding places, which can easily be provided by being given stones and plant thickets in the tank. As in the other dwarf cichlids, the water should be slightly soft and acid, and water changes should be kept to a minimum. Food as in *A. ramirezi,* discussed above.

Other *Apistogramma* species which are often available in tropical fish shops are *A. ortmanni, A. pleurotaenia, A. kleei* and *A. klausewitzi.* Their requirements are essentially the same as those described for *A. ramirezi.*

Any discussion of dwarf cichlids cannot be concluded without mentioning one of the very earliest imported forms, the striped or golden-eyed dwarf cichlid, *Nannacara anomala*. This 8 cm long fish originated in western Guyana and was first collected in 1905. It is an attractive fish where the female displays frequently changing color patterns. Males are characterized by their larger size and very strongly developed fins (longer and tips often thread-like). Among the dwarf cichlids this is the most suitable species for a community and for the beginning aquarist. It places little if any demands on water quality, as long as the water temperature falls into the range of 22° to 28° C. Food as in *A. ramirezi*, discussed above.

LABYRINTHFISHES (FAMILY BELONTIIDAE)

Members of the family occur in tropical and sub-tropical regions of Africa and especially in Southeast Asia. They inhabit primarily standing waters with dense underwater vegetation. Some even live in muddy and oxygen-poor water. All are equipped with an accessory respiratory organ, the so-called *labyrinth*, which enables them to take in air at the water surface. Therefore, labyrinthfishes can live in water which is extremely deficient in oxygen. However, they will also take air from the surface in those waters which have an adequate oxygen supply, and so not all of their required oxygen can be taken in over the gills.

Some species have their pelvic fins drawn out into a fine thread and in a very forward position. These act as a supplementary taste organ ("feeler").

Many of the labyrinthfishes make excellent aquarium fishes, since they are hardy and peaceful and many are very colorful, all-in-all an ideal combination for perfect community tank specimens.

In fact, the oldest aquarium fish, the paradisefish, *Macropodus opercularis*, is among them. This fish was first imported into France in 1869 and then to Germany in 1876. It originates in eastern and southeastern Asia (Korea, China, Vietnam and Taiwan). It is one of the hardiest aquarium

(1) A male betta tends to its brood. When the young reach this stage of development the male should be removed from the breeding tank, as he may eat the fry. (2) The blue or three-spot gourami, *Trichogaster trichopterus* should be kept with fishes its own size, as it does have a fairly rough temperament. (3) A pair of bettas in a spawning embrace. Photos 1 and 3 by H.J. Richter.

fishes around, and thus it is most suitable for the beginning aquarist. It thrives even in very small tanks and it can tolerate extremely low (for tropical fish) temperatures (range 15° to 30° C). Sometimes it is aggressive towards other tank inhabitants, and so it is often better to keep paradisefish separately and not in a community tank. Females have less intense coloration than males, and their fins are shorter (i.e. the dorsal and anal fins are not elongated).

This fish breeds very easily in captivity. Like all labyrinthfishes, the male builds a bubble nest at the surface (ideally among floating plants or leaves from submerged plants reaching the surface) into which the eggs are deposited. The nest is guarded by the male until the young leave it. This fish prefers a densely planted tank, ideally with a fair amount of algal growth. It is truly omnivorous, feeding on all available dried and live foods.

The most popular anabantid, if not one of the most popular of all aquarium fishes, is the Siamese fighting fish, *Betta splendens*. It grows to a length of about 6 cm and originates from the Malay Peninsula and from Thailand. It too is one of the earliest aquarium fishes to be imported. Since the males are extremely aggressive towards each other (fighting fish) only one male should be kept in each tank, together with several females if breeding is desired. From the relativley drab, short-finned wild form a number of long-finned forms in a variety of spectacular colors have been bred. These (males) should always be kept in separate small tanks arranged so that they can see each other. Because of the extreme aggressiveness of males (they will even attack their own image in a mirror), this species is used in contests in southeastern Asia. It should be kept fairly warm (26° to 32° C). The tank should be well planted and should not be too high, with a low water level. Although a male and some females can be kept in a community tank, these fish do best and look more effective when kept in separate tanks. Food as indicated for *Macropodus opercularis*, above.

Another very popular labyrinthfish is the dwarf gourami, *Colisa lalia*. It grows to about 5 cm and comes from India. This too is a very beautiful and peaceful little fish which does well in any community tank. The tank should be densely planted, otherwise it tends to be very shy and goes easily into hiding. The males can easily be recognized by their brighter colors (in adults) and long, extended dorsal and anal fins. These are rounded off in females. This fish breeds very easily in captivity, where the male builds the typical bubble nest, guards it after spawning and looks after the young. It tends to be very aggressive towards the female after spawning has taken place, so it is advisable to use a large (30-gallon) tank or simply remove the female. The ideal water temperature falls between 20° and 27° C. The dwarf gourami is not particular about the type of water it is in. Feed as indicated for *Macropodus opercularis*, above.

Very similar in biology and aquarium requirements is the thick-lipped gourami, *Colisa labiosa,* which is also commonly available in tropical fish stores and can also be readily kept in a community tank.

A somewhat larger fish is the pearl gourami, *Trichogaster leeri,* which grows to about 15 cm. It comes originally from the Malay Peninsula, Thailand and the Sunda Islands. This is a very attractive and peaceful fish, but unfortunately it tends to be a bit shy and quickly goes into hiding when disturbed. Males are characterized by an extended dorsal and anal fin and, as in all gouramis, the pelvic fins are vastly prolonged into a long, thin thread. These can be moved independently and act as "feelers." A closely related form is the moonlight gourami, *Trichogaster microlepis,* a 15 cm long fish from Thailand. Both fishes (as indeed all gouramis) require reasonably high temperatures (23° to 30° C) for their well-being and, in particular, for breeding. These two gouramis are quite suitable for a community tank, but they are more effectively displayed when kept by themselves in a separate tank. The tank should be densely planted and have a cover of floating plants. Feed as indicated for *Macropodus opercularis,* above.

For many years another gourami, the three-spot gourami, *Trichogaster trichopterus,* was also a "staple" in most fish stores' inventories, but it appears to have given way to a couple of more attractive domesticated forms, the "Cosby variety" and a golden form. The aquarium requirements for both are essentially the same as discussed for the other gouramis listed above.

Opposite: Plants such as the giant val, *Vallisneria gigantea,* make an excellent background plant or centerpiece plant for a very tall aquarium. To flourish, this plant needs very strong illumination. Photo by T.J. Horeman.
Below: A dense background of aquarium plants helps highlight the iridescent colors in fishes such as these *Rasbora pauciperforata.* Photo by Dr. D. Terver, Nancy Aquarium, France.

Plants

Although water plants play a vital role in the aquatic ecosystem, in an aquarium their role is invariably reduced to serve merely as decoration. To a lesser degree water plants help to maintain the biological balance by utilizing the harmful waste products of the fishes. An essential part of this process is the intake, by the plants, of carbon dioxide given off during the respiration of fishes. The plants utilize this to produce new plant tissue and for the output of oxygen. In fishes this process is reversed; they take in oxygen during respiration and give off carbon dioxide.

This intake (assimilation) of carbon dioxide by plants can only take place under the influence of light (daylight or artificial). At other times plants too will use oxygen; this is an important point to remember. A densely planted aquarium will have to be aerated at night.

In addition, water plants absorb nutrients (inorganic salts) from the water, which may be derived from decayed foods and fish feces; these substances are potentially dangerous to fishes. However, plants take in only very small amounts of them and this process is of no real significance in an aquarium situation.

If aquarium plants are to do well they will have to be given sufficient light, which can either be daylight or artificial. Daylight easily provides too much illumination, which tends to encourage unattractive green algal growth. Moreover, certain plants require fairly low levels of light intensity, so that it is easier to use artificial light sources.

Water plant culture has been made much easier in recent years by the introduction of special fluorescent light tubes for aquarium use. They are sold under various trade names, but all of them emit light in wave lengths which promote plant growth without encouraging the growth of algae.

Acorus

This is a very sturdy marsh plant from Asia. It can be kept under water but will grow only slowly. For better growth the soil should contain peat and clay, which is often very difficult to do in an aquarium situation. But even without this supplement this is a very enduring, tough plant which even plant-eating fishes will not attack. Growth occurs through additional leaves from a common root stock.

Anubias

This is another marsh and swamp plant, this one from central and west Africa. It has a "creeping" widely branched root stock and pointed leaves which can be kept sub-

76

merged but it will only grow rather slowly under these conditions. According to aquarium experience *Anubias nana* is the most suitable species.

Aponogeton

This is a large group of true underwater plants, and many species have become very popular aquarium plants. These plants are widespread throughout the tropics of the "Old World"; they are absent from the Americas. Most *Aponogeton* species require a regular rest period; the leaves die off and the bulb remains in the bottom soil for three weeks to four months (depending upon the species). This period coincides with a drop in temperature, and the most attractive specimens are grown when the rest period is being maintained. Many newly imported *Aponogeton* plants have been lost by having been kept constantly at high temperatures. Some of the more common ones are *A. ulvaceus* and *A. crispus.* The well-known Madagascar lace plant, *A. fenestralis,* lacks tissue between the leaf veins, giving it the "lacy" appearance. Most *Aponogeton* species prefer soft, slightly acid water, with a bottom soil rich in nutrients.

Bacopa

This is a swamp and marsh plant with representatives in North America and Southeast Asia. The American species *B. amplexicaulis* occurs throughout the Atlantic coastal states. It has oval leaves arranged around a center stem, and it is a very attractive aquarium plant.

Cabomba

The various *Cabomba* species are among the most attractive aquarium plants. They occur in the southeastern United States, throughout Central America and into South America. Most tropical forms prefer soft water and temperatures from 23° to 25° C, and never below about 18° C. Illumination should be fairly bright (artificial), but direct ex-

1

Cryptocoryne cordata (1), *Echinodorus bleheri,* commonly known as the Amazon sword plant (2), and *Aponogeton echinotus* (3) all make excellent centerpiece plants. Neutral to slightly alkaline water suits these plants well, but the Amazon sword plant and the *Aponogeton* require much stronger illumination than the *Cryptocoryne* does. (4) *Cabomba caroliniana* is commonly used as a background plant. Photos by R. Zukal.

posure to sun tends to promote excessive algal growth on these delicately branched plants.

Ceratopteris

Morphologically this is a highly variable water plant which occurs in all tropical regions. It can be grown submerged (planted in soil), but once the leaves reach the water surface small off-shoots will be separated off the main leaves and continue their existence as floating plants. The leaf shape and form vary, depending on whether the plant grows submerged or free-floating. It is attractively bright green and a very popular aquarium plant.

This plant, often referred to as "water fern," requires a fair amount of light and should be kept rather warm (23° to 26° C). Development comes to a halt at temperatures below 18° C.

Cryptocoryne

This is a rather large group (more than 60 known species) of mostly leafy plants which occur throughout Southeast Asia and the Sunda Islands. Many are marsh and swamp plants, and even those growing totally submerged grow slowly. Most species are very dark (green), indicating that they grow in rather shaded areas (avoiding direct sunlight). For most efficient growth cryptocorynes require soft and slightly acid water. These plants are rather susceptible to some serious diseases, especially when they are being transplanted.

Echinodorus (Sword Plants)

This is a diverse group of underwater and marsh plants, with many species not yet very well identified and understood. Many species become very large with attractive bright green leaves, and they are most suitable as aquarium plants for large tanks (although several dwarf species are also commercially available). They require a fair amount of light. Most species are not particular about the type of water they are being kept in.

Elodea

This is a very cosmopolitan group of water plants which occurs in all temperate and tropical waters. Several species are very popular aquarium plants, and they are excellent for beginning aquarists. These plants grow rapidly under almost any condition and give off much oxygen. They can be either planted or be left free-floating.

Myriophyllum

This is a cosmopolitan type of plant commonly referred to as water milfoil by aquarists. It is fast growing and has considerable decorative value. Because of its finely divided branches it is an excellent spawning medium for egglaying fishes.

Sagittaria

These plants are commonly referred to as arrowheads because of their long, narrow and pointed leaves. They are excellent aquarium plants, where they grow rapidly under almost any conditions. Most species can grow as both submerged plants and as swamp and marsh plants.

Vallisneria

This group of plants is distributed over four continents, where it occurs in temperate to tropical waters. These plants are very similar to *Sagittaria,* but can be distinguished from these by the arrangement of the leaf veins. However, usually *Vallisneria* has narrower leaves, and in several species these are growing is a spiral shape. They are hardy aquarium plants and are espeically useful for the beginning aquarist. They propagate by sending out "runners" and, under the right conditions, they tend to be very prolific. They are undemanding plants which will grow in nearly any kind of soil and even under marginal light conditions. Ideally the temperature should not fall below 18° C. *Vallisneria* species are widely available in tropical fish stores, and at low prices.

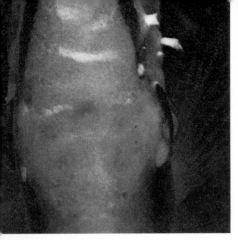

The discus (opposite) is suffering from hexamitiasis, better known as hole-in-the-head disease. The disease is caused by a flagellated protozoan called *Hexamita* (below). This disease is reported commonly by the owners of larger fishes and is not easy to cure. Photos by Frickhinger.

Diseases

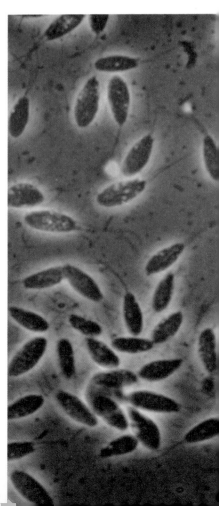

Fishes are just as prone to diseases as are other living organisms, diseases which are caused by bacteria, viruses and a multitude of other organisms. In addition, diseases in fishes can also be caused by malnutrition, poisoning or simple stress, such as overcrowding.

QUARANTINE

It is of paramount importance for every aquarist to realize that *all* newly acquired fishes must be quarantined BEFORE they are introduced into the aquarium. Irrespec-

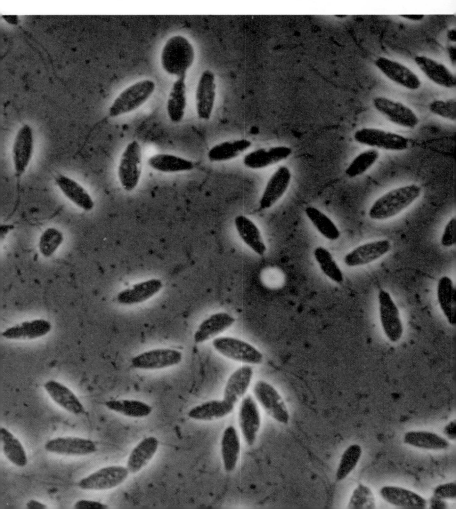

African cichlids are frequent victims of finrot, as they are constantly chasing one another and nipping each other's fins. The white edge along the shredded fins indicates that these fishes are being attacked by a species of fungus. This condition can be avoided, even when the fishes do have fin damage, by maintaining a very clean aquarium environment. Photo by A. Ivanoff.

tive of the source of his fish, the aquarist cannot know whether these are carriers of disease organisms. So, how can we find out whether newly purchased fishes are free from diseases and other organic problems? They must be isolated in a separate quarantine tank for a period of about a week or so.

During that time we observe our fishes closely to see whether they show any disease symptoms or other abnormalities. Fishes which persistently have their dorsal and caudal fins folded are likely to be sick. If, in addition, they "hang" close to the surface "gasping," then there is a definite problem and remedies have to be applied immediately. Similarly, the refusal of food for a prolonged (several days) period of time also makes a fish suspect of having something wrong with it.

POISONING

Poisoning symptoms are often rather difficult to pinpoint because metallic poisons (copper, mercury, etc.) are cumulative poisons, which build up very gradually in a fish's body, and thus symptoms emerge only gradually. However, poisoning can also occur through a buildup of ammonia (a waste product from the excretions of fishes). This invariably causes "gasping" at the surface and can be quickly corrected by liberal changes of water. Incidentally, most fresh water supplies throughout the world are now sterilized by the addition of chlorine, which is also a serious fish poison. To remove chlorine, water should be boiled or strongly aerated (to drive out the chlorine) or simply be left standing (in sunlight if possible) for a few days before it is used. Metal poisoning is hard to detect, and by the time definite symptoms are noticeable, the fish is, unfortunately, already beyond recovery. A rapid water change might be recommended as a "last ditch" effort, which may bring some positive results.

The white spots on the fins of this small tetra are cysts of *Ichthyophthirius multifiliis.* The disease is commonly known as "ich." It can be cured with the use of malachite green, but fishes such as tetras may require a very mild dose because of their high sensitivity to the chemical. Elevation of the temperature to 86° F. will also rid the fish of the disease. Either treatment must be sustained for about 10 days, even if the fishes look as though they have been cured long before that. Otherwise, the disease will return. Photo by R. Zukal.

3

(1) Large cichlids such as this *Aequidens rivulatus* (commonly known as the green terror) require plenty of space, for they reach a length of over 12 inches and have an extremely pugilistic temperament. Photo by H. Ross Brock. (2) The Texas cichlid, *Cichlasoma cyanoguttatum*, is the only known native American cichlid. Photo by H.J. Richter. (3) The African jewel cichlid, although not exceptionally large for a cichlid, has one of the nastiest temperaments of all of the cichlids. Here a male tends to his brood of youngsters.

OVERFEEDING AND OVERCROWDING

One of the easiest traps to fall into as a beginning aquarist is to overfeed, that is, to give more food than is eaten within a reasonably short period of time. Continuous overfeeding results in a build-up of bacteria (cloudiness) which, of course, also use the oxygen in the tank (thus depriving the fish of it) and give off toxic waste products. Unless quick corrective action is taken, the water begins to smell foul, and fish start to die. Therefore, it is better to feed more often, but smaller quantities, than to feed only once with a large amount. Aquarists must take their time when feeding and watch all fish to make sure everyone gets its share and

Undergravel filtration utilizes bacterial action to break down organic matter and render it into harmless nitrates. However, overfeeding in an aquarium can cause the gravel bed to become plugged up.

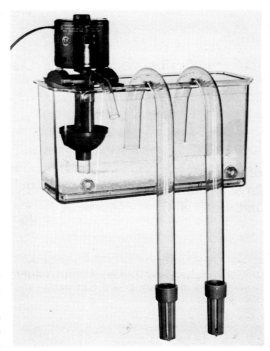

Even a strong power filter cannot compensate for overfeeding and overcrowding in an aquarium. In addition, excess food rotting in the filter box can contribute to the chemical poisoning of the aquarium's residents.

that no food accumulates on the bottom. Uneaten food must be removed (siphoned out) immediately.

Somewhat similar effects occur when a tank becomes overcrowded by too many fishes. The dissolved oxygen level drops and fishes start "gasping" at the surface for oxygen. In addition, too many fishes in a tank cause trauma and stress, which tends to weaken fish sufficiently to become easily susceptible to diseases. Moreover, too many fish in a tank have adverse effects on the water chemistry in the tank. In addition to a lowering of oxygen content and a build-up of carbon dioxide, the pH often drops to dangerous levels. In part, these problems can be solved by an improved efficiency of the filtration system together with more frequent water changes. However, the ultimate solution is a reduction in the number of fishes kept in that tank.

Many of the African mouthbrooding cichlids are much more colorful than their substrate-brooding Latin American counterparts and can withstand much more crowding. The mouthbrooders shown here are (1) *Pseudotropheus "eduardi,"* (2) *Pseudotropheus "chameleo,"* (3) *Pseudotropheus zebra* and (4) *Pseudotropheus aurora.* Photo 1 by B. Baymiller. Photos 2 and 4 by A. Norman. Photo 3 by Ken Lucas, Steinhart Aquarium.

2

3

4

BACTERIAL DISEASES

There are a great many fish diseases caused by a variety of bacteria. Invariably, the symptoms are hemorrhaging (bleeding) areas of the body and several "rotting" fins. If indeed a bacterial disease is present a prompt and persistent treatment with antibiotics will often eliminate the problem.

PROTOZOAN DISEASES

A number of serious fish diseases are being caused by protozoans, tiny single-celled organisms. The most dreaded of these is white spot or ich, *Ichthyophthirius multifiliis*, which can wipe out a whole aquarium in a short period of time. This disease is recognized by the presence of large white granular spots, ½ to 1 mm in diameter, on the body and on the fins. These spots cause considerable irritation to the fishes, which tend to "rub" their sides along the bottom or on plants, rocks, etc. in order to obtain relief.

The parasite lies under the outer skin layer of the fish. After some time it bores its way out of the fish again, falls to the bottom and divides into many tiny individuals, which immediately swim around in search of a new host fish. If they do not find a host within a few days the young parasites will die. It is very difficult to attack (treat) this parasite when it is embedded in the host's tissue, therefore any treatment has to be aimed at the free-swimming stage. A number of treatments are commercially available from pet shops. It is important that the accompanying instructions be followed closely, particularly as far as the duration of the treatment is concerned. It often helps to raise the temperature (to about 32° C) to speed up the life cycle of the parasite.

FUNGAL INFECTIONS

Fish often become injured when caught, transferred to shipping containers and ultimately into a new aquarium. Such injuries range from the loss of a few scales to severely torn fins. These wounds often are prone to secondary infections (invasions) by fungi. These can easily be recognized by small "fluffy" whitish growths on these areas and if left uncontrolled can cause the death of a fish. Fortunately, fungal diseases usually respond quickly and effectively to treatments with inorganic dyes (methylene blue, malachite green). Unfortunately, these dyes turn the water rather unsightly, stain the tank glass and kill plants. It is imperative that any treatment with these agents be made exactly according to instructions supplied.

The preceding text gives a cursory overview and basic requirements to set up and operate a home aquarium and the fishes which are available and their care and maintenance. Of course, there are many more tropical fish species which are available, however, and many of these require more specific attention. A description and discussion of these would exceed the introductory level of this book. Moreover, as the subject of tropical fish-keeping becomes more complex, so do the problems. The main problem is the very comprehensive subject of fish diseases, their recognition, treatment and prevention. Once the beginning aquarium hobbyist has reached this level, he may well wish to consult some of the more comprehensive books written on this subject. Similarly, there are now special books and booklets dealing in depth with specific groups or families of fishes and their own particular problems (and solutions to these). This little book is merely intended to guide the beginning aquarist through the first few difficult steps and help him avoid some of the obvious "pitfalls." This way he can enjoy the fruits of his efforts (and investment) without becoming discouraged. If he indeed succeeds and enjoys his new-found hobby, his innate curiosity will no doubt lead him to seek more information and knowledge about the fascinating and colorful world of tropical fishes.